FANTASTIC SPORTS

In-line SKATING

ALDIE CHALMERS

ALADDIN/WATTS
LONDON • SYDNEY

This edition printed in 2000

© Aladdin Books Ltd 1997

*Designed and
produced by*
Aladdin Books Ltd
28 Percy Street
London
W1P 0LD

ISBN 0 7496 3892 3 (paperback)

*First published in Great Britain
in 1997 by*
Aladdin Books/Watts Books
96 Leonard Street
London
EC2A 4XD

Editor
Sarah Levete

Design
David West
Children's Book Design

Designer
Flick Killerby

Illustrator
Catherine Ward – Simon Girling &
Associates

Picture Research
Brooks Krikler Research

This title was previously published in
hardcover as the Fantastic Fold-out
Book of In-line Skating

ISBN 0 7496 2884 7 (hardback)

Equipment and models supplied by
Skaters Paradise

The author, Aldie Chalmers, is an
experienced in-line skater, instructor
and writer.

Printed in Belgium

C O N T E N T S

Introduction

In-line skating is one of the world's fastest growing sports. Join the millions of people, of every age and type, who enjoy the exercise and exhilaration of in-line skating.

Today's in-line skates are made with the most up-to-date technological materials and know-how. Roller skates, or "quads", have been transformed from bulky skates with wheels arranged in a rectangle into compact, light, streamlined skates, with the wheels arranged in a straight line.

Whether or not you are an experienced skater, this book tells you everything you need to know about in-line skating from care of your skates to styling big airs, or jumps. When you are confident with the basic steps to get you moving, try some more advanced moves and tricks. But whatever your level, only try new moves when you are confident and sure that you can safely practise them.

In-line skating is fun but it is also a demanding sport. Every skater should wear full protective clothing to stay safe and to get the most from in-line skating.

Read this book – put on your pads, helmet and skates – and get rolling!

4

Taking up in-line skating

Today, in-line skating is a serious sport for professional in-line skaters as well as an extremely popular recreational activity. There are several types of in-line skating – the skates and equipment for each type have become very specialised.

If you are taking up the sport for the first time, begin as a general or "recreational" skater, or "rec" for short. You can then decide if you want to try another style of skating – "aggressive", freestyle, hockey or speed skating. Whichever form of in-line skating you take up, you are guaranteed to have fun.

"REC" AND FREESTYLE
"Rec" skating forms the large group of all skaters. It's about having fun and enjoying the thrill of free-wheeling. The m advanced form of "rec" is freestyle – new moves and tricks, often performed to dance music.

SOME REASONS TO START IN-LINE SKATING...
If you are in any doubt about why in-line skating is so popular, then read on. Readers of an international skating magazine wrote in saying why they began in-line skating.

" *There's all the fun of skiing but no need for snow; all the fun of ice skating without the need for ice... All you need is your skates, your protective gear and some space... I'm addicted to the buzz... It's for girls and boys... It's for all ages... I live on my skates, they never leave my feet... It's exhilarating... It's the best sport I've ever tried... There's so many ways to use your skates – "aggressive", hockey, speed, recreation and fitness, or just as a cool form of transportation... It's a great way to get to school... It's brilliant to skate with friends... The whole family can do it... You can just do it for fun or take it all the way to the world championships! "*

RACES FOR FUN
Everyone can enjoy skating just for fun or at a more competitive level.

Why not join in a "rat race"? You pay a small registration fee to enter a race with other people of your age. Both in-line and quad skaters are racing to the finish line in a rat race (left).

BEGIN AT THE BEGINNING

To begin with, all you need is a pair of in-line skates, the protective clothing and an empty space. But in-line skates and the necessary equipment can be expensive so, if you have not previously tried in-line skating, you can hire the skates and equipment before buying them.

Many beginners also benefit from having some lessons with a qualified in-line skating instructor. This can prevent you from picking up any bad skating habits. In-line skating magazines will have the latest news of competitions, moves and in-line skating associations. Contact your national association for the names and addresses of recommended instructors.

TING FOR EVERYONE

by your skating with a group of others *(above)* n your own. Hockey, on in-line skates or quads), is a great team sport. Why not form a team your friends and enter a league? Or join a d skating club where you can compete and with others – and have a good time. "Aggressive" ers often form a "posse" or "crew" to tise, or "session", and compete together *(right)*. take your skating to a more serious level n with local league competitions and progress ational and international competitions. There urrently world championship events for in-line d and "aggressive" skating and in-line hockey.

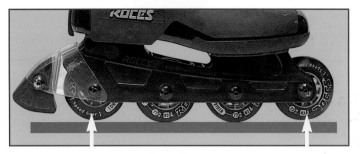

"Rockered" system

"Anti-rockered" system

ROCKING AND ROLLING

On most skates you can adjust the height of your wheels to create different skating effects. Lower the two centre wheels to create a "rockering" effect which allows you to turn more effectively.

With all the wheels flat, you can turn less easily, you gain more speed. Raise the two middle whee or replace them with smaller wheels for "anti-rockering". "Aggressive" skaters use this to "lock better to rails when grinding.

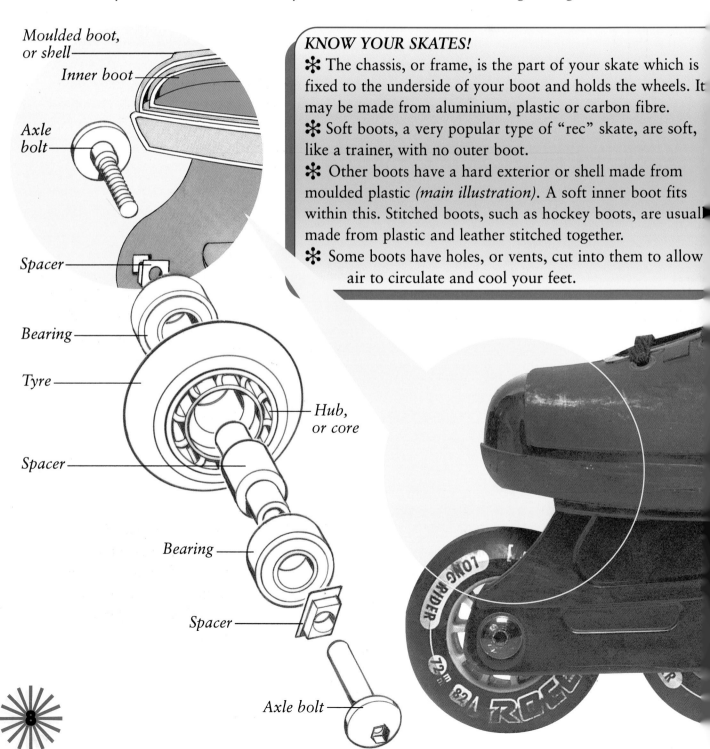

Moulded boot, or shell

Inner boot

Axle bolt

Spacer

Bearing

Tyre

Spacer

Hub, or core

Bearing

Spacer

Axle bolt

KNOW YOUR SKATES!

✳ The chassis, or frame, is the part of your skate which is fixed to the underside of your boot and holds the wheels. It may be made from aluminium, plastic or carbon fibre.

✳ Soft boots, a very popular type of "rec" skate, are soft, like a trainer, with no outer boot.

✳ Other boots have a hard exterior or shell made from moulded plastic *(main illustration)*. A soft inner boot fits within this. Stitched boots, such as hockey boots, are usual made from plastic and leather stitched together.

✳ Some boots have holes, or vents, cut into them to allow air to circulate and cool your feet.

8

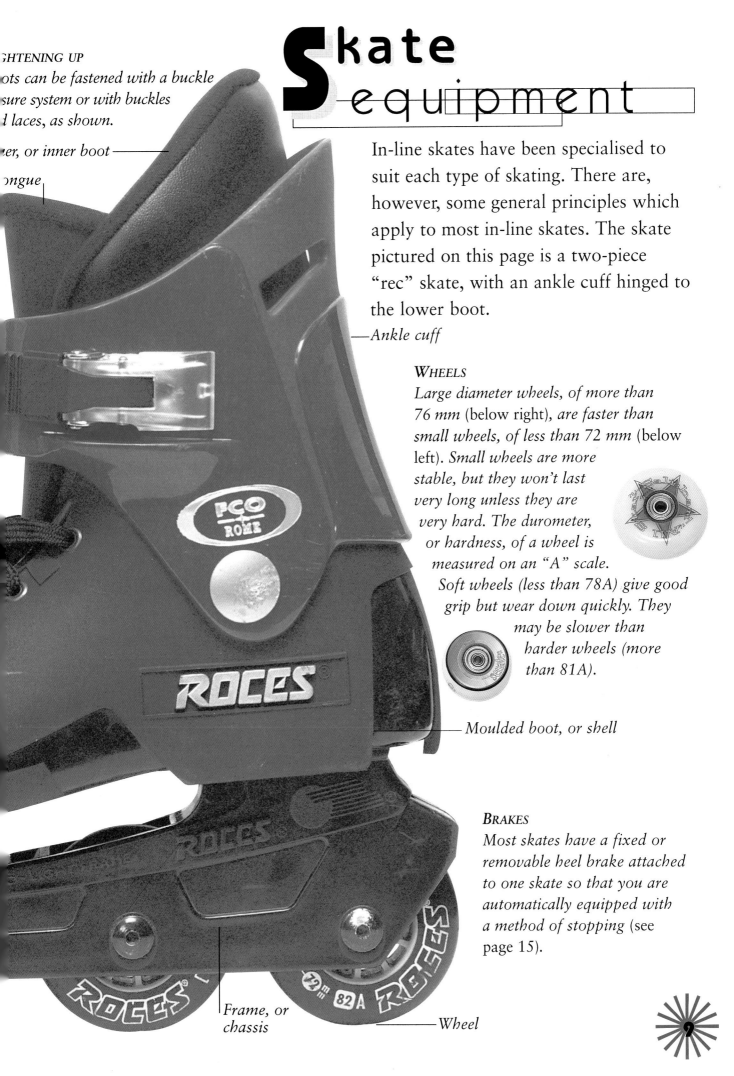

Skate equipment

GHTENING UP

ots can be fastened with a buckle
sure system or with buckles
d laces, as shown.

er, or inner boot ——————

ongue

In-line skates have been specialised to suit each type of skating. There are, however, some general principles which apply to most in-line skates. The skate pictured on this page is a two-piece "rec" skate, with an ankle cuff hinged to the lower boot.

—*Ankle cuff*

WHEELS

Large diameter wheels, of more than 76 mm (below right), are faster than small wheels, of less than 72 mm (below left). Small wheels are more stable, but they won't last very long unless they are very hard. The durometer, or hardness, of a wheel is measured on an "A" scale.
Soft wheels (less than 78A) give good grip but wear down quickly. They may be slower than harder wheels (more than 81A).

———— *Moulded boot, or shell*

BRAKES

Most skates have a fixed or removable heel brake attached to one skate so that you are automatically equipped with a method of stopping (see page 15).

Frame, or chassis

—*Wheel*

Skate gear for safety

Skating on hard surfaces can do a lot of damage to your elbows, knees and your head if you fall. It is important to pad up before you even put your skates on. Try to get the best protective clothing that you can afford – the better the equipment, the more it will protect you. Wearing pads actually helps you to skate better because it gives you the confidence to skate safely. Remember, if you fall you want to graze the plastic of your pads, NOT your soft flesh.

SHORTS
A bit of extra padding can make all the difference if you fall! Wear trousers or baggy shorts which are fitted with extra padding (below) for your hips and your backside. If you wear tracksuit bottoms or leggings, sew in some thick foam to create extra padding.

SAVE YOUR HEAD
You can buy specialist in-line skating helmets (above) from most skate shops. Make sure that the helmet is the right size for your head, and wear it – it's your only head!

LOOKS GOOD
Elbows are very vulnerable and must be protected with elbow pads (above). Wrist guards (right) look cool – and they protect your wrists

Safety doesn't just mean protective clothing. It means following the rules of the road (below right). If you think you may be skating when it gets dark, take your lights with you. Attach a light to the back of your helmet – check the batteries before you set out. Buy lights which clip onto your boots (left), or attach regular bike lights with some stick-on Velcro strips. Wear a reflective band or strip across your body – the brighter the better!

If you fall, you should fall forwards onto your knees (see page 13). Protect your knees with well-fitting knee pads (below).

RULES OF THE ROAD

Look after yourself and others when you are out skating:

✳ Always wear the correct protective clothing and make sure you have lights and reflective strips for skating in the dark.

✳ Make sure your equipment is in good working order.

✳ Always tell an adult where you are going to be skating and at what time you will be back.

✳ Only skate in areas where it is allowed. Avoid traffic. Where permission is given to skate in a car park, make sure it is not in use.

✳ Show consideration to pedestrians.

✳ Observe all the traffic regulations. If you don't, you put yourself and others at great risk.

CHOOSE CAREFULLY!

Make sure that you use skates which are appropriate to the style of your in-line skating. You will be very uncomfortable if your boots don't fit, so make sure you get the right size. Your foot should feel secure but not restricted within your boot – you should be able to wiggle your toes. Spend as much time as you need when you buy or hire a pair of skates – otherwise you will be uncomfortable, and your skating will suffer.

STRETCH YOUR CHEST
Interlock your hands behind your body. Extend your arms behind you and raise them upwards slightly.

STRETCH YOUR UPPER BACK
Interlock your hands and stretch your arms out in front of you. Repeat the exercise, but with your palms turned away from your body.

STRETCH YOUR UPPER THIGHS
Stand on one leg with your knee slightly bent. Bend your other leg back. Hold your ankle with your hand. Keeping your knees together, pull your raised leg towards your backside. Push your foot against your hand.

STRETCH THE BACK OF YOUR THIGHS
Extend one leg forwards. Bend the other leg slightly, placing your hands lightly on your upper thigh. Bring your weight over your extended leg.

STRETCH YOUR HIPS
Extend one leg backwards, placing your knee on the floor. Bend your other leg in front of you. Bring your weight slightly forwards, keeping the knee of your front leg at a right angle to your foot.

STRETCH YOUR INNER THIGHS
Sit upright with your legs apart and your hands in front of your body. Gently press forwards, keeping your legs extended.

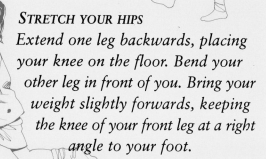

WARM UP AND STRETCH
Stretching *(left)* reduces the chances of injury or strain to your body. It also increases your flexibility (the range of movement in your body) and improves your performance. It is important warm up gradually. Always stretch slowly and never bounce in a stretch. And don't forget to stretch both legs!

Getting started

You've got the skates, you've got the gear now get going – on your stretches! Skatin is a physical activity so you should alway warm up and stretch before doing it first

When you first start skating, your skate will feel very strange. Practise the technic for getting up safely. Once you are up, make sure you always adopt a good read position. You will inevitably fall over at some point in your skating career – so learn how to fall safely.

1

GETTING UP
Get up the easy and safe way! Bend down on your hands and knees, with the toes of your skates touching the ground 1 . Bring one forwards (keeping it bent) so that the whee of the skate are in contact with the ground.

LEARNING HOW TO FALL

You should try to fall the shortest distance possible, which is forwards onto your knee pads. If your knees are bent before the fall, the impact or force with which you hit the ground is greatly reduced. When you fall forwards try to protect your head and face. The best position is on your elbow pads with your hands outstretched in front of you *(below left)*.

Try to avoid falling backwards – because you'll have further to fall. However, if you do fall backwards, don't try to get your hands under your body to break the fall because you may well injure your wrists. Instead, try to twist at the waist so that the top half of your body is facing the direction of the fall *(right)*. But, as you already know, falling safely can only be safe if you are wearing the correct protective clothing.

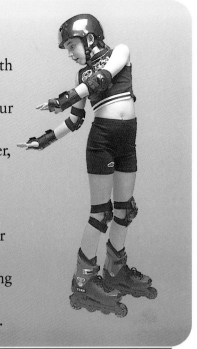

...en you first practise getting up, ...d on to a stable post or bar ...h one hand.

2

3

4

...e both your hands on your raised knee 2 . ...port your weight with your hands on your ...ed knee. As you straighten the raised leg, you ...come to a standing position 3 . Keep your ...slightly bent and your weight slightly ...wards 4 . This is your basic ready position.

IN POSITION
When you first wear skates, you may want to stand upright. However, the ready position (knees bent and weight slightly forwards) will help you keep your balance and stop you falling backwards. Very skilled skaters, who may skate with their knees straight, adopt the ready position just before stopping, or when they wish to become more stable.

In the ready position bring your feet to a "V" shape. Point both skates outwards ⬚1 .

Raise your right skate slightly and place it in fron[t] you. Your weight is on your left trailing skate ⬚2

Direction of travel

Moving forwards

Don't just kit up, aim yourself down the road and go – that's the best way to have a nasty accident. Start with the "duck" walk on grass or on a thick carpet.

When you become used to the feel of this, practise striding on your skates. This is like the "duck" walk but, instead of lifting up your skates, you use a stroking and gliding movement. When you move forwards you steer with your front, or leading, skate – it is positioned in the direction in which you are travelling. You push and thrust with your back, or trailing, skate. Remember, if you lean backwards you will stop moving forwards – but you will start to fall backwards!

Bring your left skate through th[e] "V" position ⬚3 ; place it in fr[ont] of you ⬚4 . Repeat steps 1-4. Th[en] the "duck" walk.

14

First practise on grass.

STROKING AND GLIDING

From the "V" position, thrust back and slightly out to the side with the trailing skate. As you do so, momentarily transfer your weight from the front skate to the trailing skate, shown by the blue triangle *(left)*. This stroke powers forwards movement. Transfer your weight to the front skate as you glide, or coast, on this skate. Bring your trailing foot to the front to continue the sequence. The stroking and gliding action is called striding.

stroke (see right), *thrust
 your weight from
 trailing skate.*

EL BRAKE STOP

*d a smooth, level area, free of obstacles such as twigs or
cks in the paving. Scissor your legs so that your skate with
 heel brake is in the front position. Point the toe of this
te upwards; your heel brake comes in contact with the
und. Don't try to stop straight away – bring the brake into
tact with the ground very lightly at first. Slowly add more
ssure to the heel brake. Concentrate on keeping your balance.*

A-FRAME TURN

This is a simple way to turn (above). Roll forwards slowly, taking your skates to a wide stance. Your skates point forwards. To turn to the right, shift your weight onto your left skate. Without lifting your skates off the ground, apply slight pressure to your left skate so that the heel is being pushed outwards and the toe is being pushed inwards. This will start the turn. Keep your weight and pressure on the left skate to complete the turn. Do not stroke during the turn.

RACE EVENTS

In many countries, speed skating associations organise competitions and events for all age groups and abilities. Start with a fun race (see page 7). If y enjoy it, why not join a speed club an start entering races (left)?

RACING TO THE TOP

Sutton (Sooty) Atkins, shown in the lead (*above left*), is one of Britain's top speed skat When he discovered t thrills of the sport he began a local speed club. He now travels world to train, compete and co

Speed skating

One of the most exciting areas of in-line skating is speed skating, a fast and demanding sport. Speed skaters can reach speeds of up to 42 kilometres per hour. Race distances vary from short sprints of 200 metres to endurance races of 100 kilometres. You can compete in races at a local club level – and if you have the skill you may even reach the World Championships.

To reduce wind resistance and therefore to increase their speed, some speed skaters may wear a Lycra cover over their skates (right).

RACING GEAR

In races speed skaters wear helmets similar to cycle helmets and streamlined Lycra "skin suits". Elbow, knee or wrist protection is not worn because these would slow down the skaters. However, all races are strictly supervised to make them as safe as possible.

TECHNIQUE

A speed skater must keep his or her body lower to the ground than that of a "rec" in-liner. being low (as shown in the illustrations), y skates are in co with the ground longer and you u achieve a longer and thrust. Speed skates very light and strong and are specially moulded to fit the skater's foot exactly! Most speed skates have a five-wheel frame which is faster than the four-wheel "rec" skate.

n-line
hockey

[...]ne hockey (or roller hockey as it is also commonly [kno]wn) is increasing in popularity. It has all the thrills and [exci]tement of ice hockey, on which it is based, but it is [play]ed on the streets, in school halls and in leisure centres [- al]most anywhere it can be played safely.

[On]ce you are confident with your basic in-line moves and stops, join in an informal game of in-line hockey, often called pick-up hockey. It's a quick and fun way to learn how to control your skates and speed.

The goalie (above) *wears more protection than other players!*

[TEA]MS

[...]ne hockey is a [team] sport *(right)*. [Mos]t forms of the [game] are played [with] four outfield [play]ers (two [attac]kers and two [defen]ders) and a [goali]e. The game [allow]s an individual [to de]monstrate his or her skills, [but t]he success of a team depends upon the ability [of th]e players to work well together.

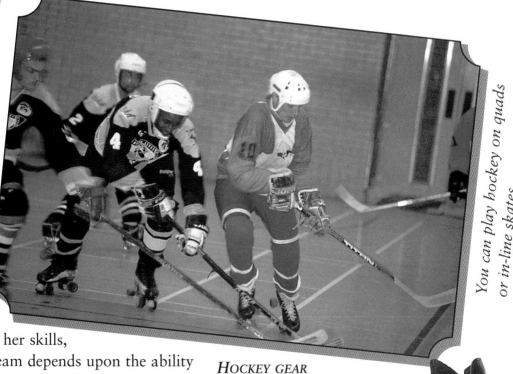

You can play hockey on quads or in-line skates.

THE BASIC GAME

[I]n-line hockey is played with a long stick [(*far right*)] made from wood or metal, and a [weighted puck, or ball. The aim of the game [i]s to put the puck into the net as many times [a]s possible. Some forms of hockey allow [p]hysical contact; others do not. In-line [h]ockey can be played in venues of all sizes.

HOCKEY GEAR
Your skates need to be as tough and as light as possible. You can buy specialised skates (right) *or you can adapt regular skates by fitting the appropriate wheels and rockering them* (see page 8). *Wear the full protective gear and a hockey helmet, ideally with a full-face shield* (above left).

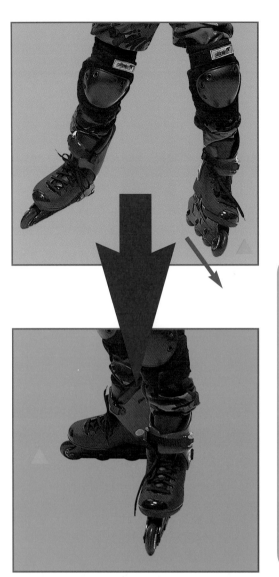

WHAT A DRAG!

*In the drag stop, or T-stop, the friction from your trailing whe[el]
slows you down. Support your weight on your front skate. T[his]
skate points in the direction in which you are moving (top lef[t].
Lower your trailing skate gently to the ground so that the wh[eels]
are at a 90° angle to the direction in which you are travelling.
Apply downward pressure with your trailing skate (below left[).*

*Use your arms and your waist to prevent you from spinning[. If]
you practise this too fast, you will spin out of control.*

HELP!

In-liners face some common problems which are
easily corrected if you follow some basic principles:
❋ Start at a very slow speed. Build up your
speed gradually. Do not try to perform any
stops at a fast speed until you can perform
them well from a slow skating speed.
❋ Use the ready position *(see pages 12-13)*
to help keep your balance as you stop.
Keep your knees bent. Don't be
tempted to lean backwards with
straight legs *(right)*.
❋ Never go faster than the speed at
which you know you can safely stop.

SPIN STOP

Practise this stop at VERY slow speeds to start with.

Take your weight onto your leading foot ①. If
you are turning to the left this will be your right
foot. If you are turning to the right this will be
your left foot. Lift the back wheel of your trailing
skate, keeping the front wheel on the ground ②.

Turn this skate to a right angle to your leading
skate. Lower it to the ground ③. As you do s[o]
your body will turn in the direction of the trail[ing]
skate ④. The spinning action will bring you t[o a]
halt ⑤. To control the movement, flex your a[rms]
and legs. Make sure that you are leaning forwa[rds]
and not backwards.

...ER SLIDE

...his variation of an impressive but ...cult move, bend both your knees ...Raise the heel of your right skate ...turn it to face outwards. Move ...weight onto this trailing foot ...his example, right foot) 2 .

Bending low, swing the left skate out in a large arc. Bring the right heel to the ground 3 . Bring your left skate to the ground at a right angle. Your left leg is straight; your right knee is bent 4 . Keep your body low.

earning to
stop!

...already know the heel brake stop *(see page 15)*, but ...re are several other ways to stop. Practise as ...ny as possible because each one will be ...ful in different situations. If you are an "aggressive" or speed ...ter, or if you play in-line hockey, you will not often use the heel ...ke stop, so it is particularly important for you to learn other forms of stopping.

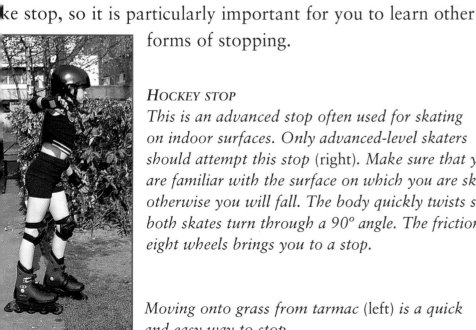

HOCKEY STOP
This is an advanced stop often used for skating on indoor surfaces. Only advanced-level skaters should attempt this stop (right). Make sure that you are familiar with the surface on which you are skating – otherwise you will fall. The body quickly twists so that both skates turn through a 90° angle. The friction of all eight wheels brings you to a stop.

Moving onto grass from tarmac (left) is a quick and easy way to stop.

19

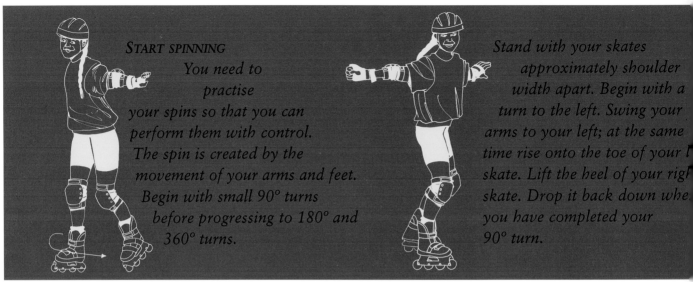

You need to practise your spins so that you can perform them with control. The spin is created by the movement of your arms and feet. Begin with small 90° turns before progressing to 180° and 360° turns.

Stand with your skates approximately shoulder width apart. Begin with a turn to the left. Swing your arms to your left; at the same time rise onto the toe of your l skate. Lift the heel of your rig skate. Drop it back down whe you have completed your 90° turn.

HEEL-TOE BALANCE

Warm up well and do an inner thigh stretch *(see page 12)* before trying this trick. Scissor your legs, supporting your weight evenly between the two. At the same time, lift the toe of your leading skate and the heel of your trailing skate *(right)*. You may find it easier to raise one skate first, and then the other when you feel comfortable. Hold this position as long as possible. If you have an attached heel brake, lift the toe of the skate without the brake, as shown.

Step 1: *Lean to the left, taking all your weight onto your left foot* 1 .

CROSS-OVER TURNS

These turns look great and they allow you take a corner without losing any speed. Yo can actually accelerate using this turn. To perform a cross-over turn, you need to dev confidence supporting all your weight on inside skate whilst leaning into the In the sequence *(above and oppos* the skater is turning to the left. T position of her weight is indica by the blue triangle. First practi this with small cross-over steps. As y gain confidence you can increase their ran

...eat all of these
...s to increase your
... to 180°.

...en you start spinning, keep
... arms outstretched to make
... turn more slowly. If you
...g your arms in closer to your
...s while you are spinning, you
... increase the speed of
... spin.

Step 3: *Bring the right skate in front of the left skate following the line of the turn. Transfer your weight onto your right foot* 3 . *Lift the left skate; bring it in front of the right skate in line with the turn.*

Repeat steps 2-3, using alternate skates, until you have completed the turn.

Advanced moves

One thing that keeps in-line skating fun is that there is always room for improvement. There is always a new trick to learn or something that you can get better at. These are some useful and fun moves that you may wish to learn.

But remember, however advanced your moves or tricks, pad up well. It doesn't look, or feel, very good if you hurt yourself.

... 2: *Lift your right skate off the
...nd, keeping your weight on
... left skate* 2 .

Step 5: *Repeat the process so that your heels are moving in and out, forming a snake-like pattern with each skate* 5 *.*

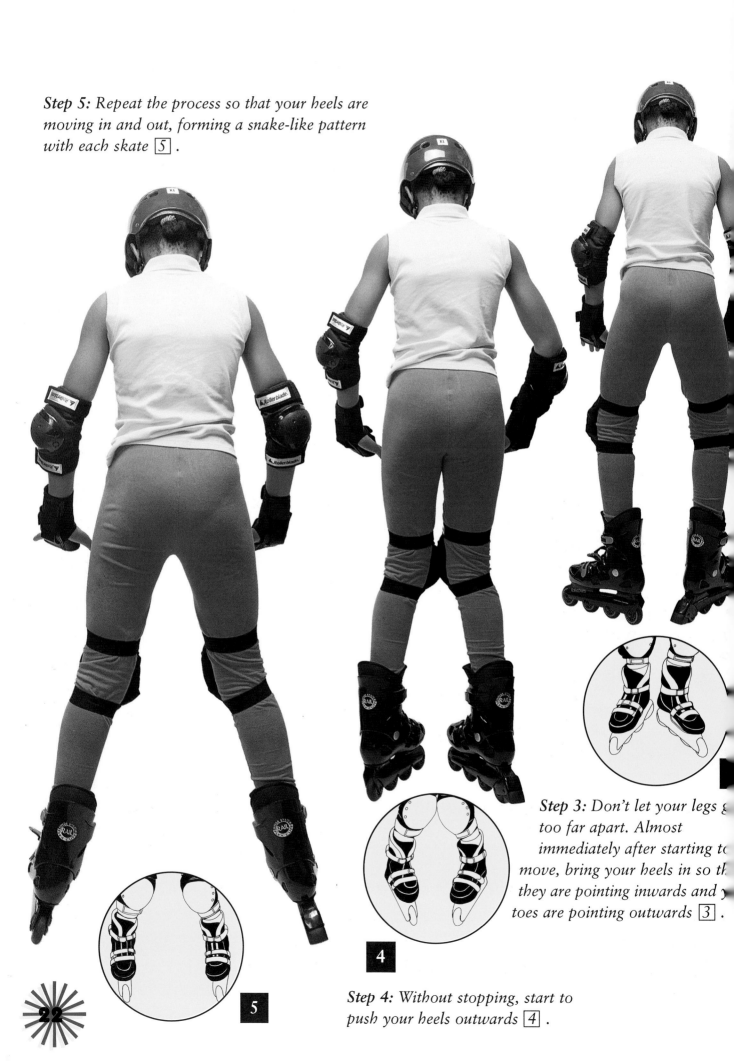

Step 3: Don't let your legs g too far apart. Almost immediately after starting t move, bring your heels in so th they are pointing inwards and toes are pointing outwards 3 .

4

5

Step 4: *Without stopping, start to push your heels outwards* 4 *.*

SKATING AT THE TOP

When an "aggressive" skater, such as Brian Smith from the USA *(below)*, makes it to the top, he or she can become a professional skater. He or she may be approached by an in-line skate company who will sponsor, or pay, the skater. In return, the skater promotes the company and its products. You can see skaters such as Brian doing the latest moves at "aggressive" events and shows.

1

Step 1: Start with the toes of your skates pointing inwards and your heels outwards. Keep your knees bent and all your wheels in contact with the ground **1** *.*

2

*2: Gently push outwards
g pressure from the front,
e, part of your skate* **2** *.*

ON ONE LEG

Improve your skating the quick way! Practising on one skate will help you with a lot of the advanced moves and stops, many of which, such as the power slide *(see page 19)*, often require you to support all of your weight on one skate. Gradually build up the distance you can skate on one leg. Try it on the other leg, too! After a while, try a snake pattern on one leg *(right)*.

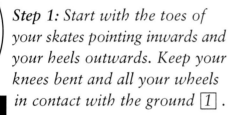

kating
backwards

rybody wants to skate backwards. It looks great – and it's fun to The backwards swizzle is the best way to learn how to skate kwards. It is also known as the "snake pattern" or the "hour-glass" ause of the pattern made by the path of your skates.

rst practise your steps without moving at speed. If you feel unsure egin with, give yourself a gentle push from a wall. When you ially start to move, look over your shoulder to check that it is safe you to start skating.

LEARNING TO JUMP
Before you actually take off, think about your landing – it is very important not to fall backwards on landing. You need to land with your legs apart and slightly scissored, and your weight slightly forwards (left).

Start your jumps from a stationary position. To begin with, aim low rather than high. Use your arms to provide the momentum to lift you off the ground. Once you feel confident about your landing technique, try taking off while moving slowly.

STAIR JUMPING

After jumping on flat surfaces, in-line skaters often progress to getting more air by launching off stairs *(below)*. But remember, start on a drop of only one or two steps and gradually build up the number of steps you can jump. When you are at an advanced level, try landing "fakie" (backwards) after turning through 180° in the air.

Styling the air

If you thought that skating only involved stroking and gliding on flat ground, think again! "Aggressive" skaters, and sometimes "rec" skaters, enjoy the thrill of using the momentum, or force, gained from rolling on skates to launch themselves into the air. Now jumping, more often known as "airing", has become a major part of "aggressive" skating with styled airs bringing high marks in competition. It spectacular, and the added difficulty of landing bi airs brings loads of thrills. Before attempting even the smallest jumps, make sure you are wearing adequate padding and your helmet.

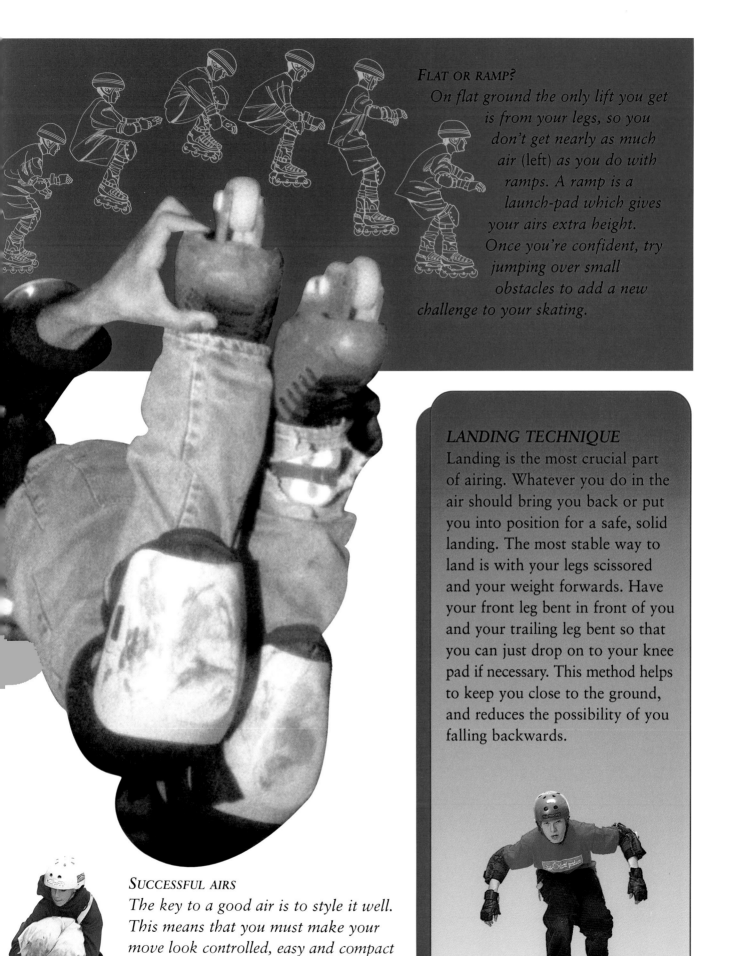

FLAT OR RAMP?

On flat ground the only lift you get is from your legs, so you don't get nearly as much air (left) as you do with ramps. A ramp is a launch-pad which gives your airs extra height. Once you're confident, try jumping over small obstacles to add a new challenge to your skating.

LANDING TECHNIQUE

Landing is the most crucial part of airing. Whatever you do in the air should bring you back or put you into position for a safe, solid landing. The most stable way to land is with your legs scissored and your weight forwards. Have your front leg bent in front of you and your trailing leg bent so that you can just drop on to your knee pad if necessary. This method helps to keep you close to the ground, and reduces the possibility of you falling backwards.

SUCCESSFUL AIRS

The key to a good air is to style it well. This means that you must make your move look controlled, easy and compact (above and left). A smaller air with a neat position is much better than a high air with arms and legs flailing. Remember, don't just air it... style it!

OFF-ROAD IN-LINE

Off-road skating is a new and popular development in in-line skating. An extra long aluminium frame with large wheels at either end *(below right)* allows skaters to travel over rough and rocky ground. Off-roaders will find a stretch of ground over which they can roll on their skates, and aim for some big airs.

CROSS-OVER TRAINING

In-line skating is an excellent, fun way to improve your training programme (left), *whatever sport you are involved in. It supplies all the exercise benefits of jogging without placing pressure on your joints. As well as being fun, skating can also be serious physical exercise.*

Other styles

line skating is an incredibly diverse
ort, ranging from speed racing *(far
t)* to "aggressive" skating *(right).*
ople are always inventing new
ys to enjoy it. Games such as
ch, bulldog, tennis, basketball and
en football take on a new twist when
u play them on wheels! In the future you
y see new developments in the sport from
-road racing to long-jump championships.

"Aggressive" skaters are kitted up and ready to go (below).

FREESTYLE

limits, no rules and any place
long as it is safe; freestyle
ting is filled with exciting
ves and sequences which are
much fun to watch as they are
erform. Freestyle is often
formed with music and has a
ce feel to it.

ENJOY IT!
The key to skating success is enjoyment! Don't worry if you are a
beginner practising your "duck" steps and another skater goes
whizzing by. Everyone has to start at the beginning! With practice
you will make progress. Whatever your level, the most important
factor must be safety for you and those around you.

If you enjoy team sports, why not join a club or a team? And if
you can't find one, start your own! It's a great way to meet new
friends and skating buddies. Skate clubs exist for everyone from
"rec" skaters to fitness fanatics and competition skaters.

IN-LINE HISTORY

Did you know that in-line skates are over 100 years old? Their predecessor, the roller skate, or quad, was developed in the 1700s and is still used today. In the 1800s, iron in-line skates were developed. Up until the 1970s only a few design improvements were made (below).

For years, people of all ages have enjoyed skating on quads.

However, in-line skates only really took off when Scott Olson, an ice-hockey player, developed a pair of skates on which he could train all year round. Modern in-liners were made – and the rest is history!

Skate care for safety

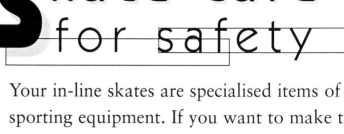

Your in-line skates are specialised items of sporting equipment. If you want to make the most of them, you will need to maintain and care for them properly. This means checking them for wear and tear and cleaning them regularly.

By looking after your skates they will last longer and perform better. They will also keep you safe.

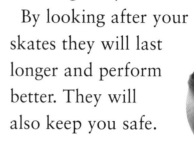

PUT YOUR BRAKES ON!

Brakes wear down from constant use. Make sure that you replace them before they reach the end of the rubber. If you have screws attaching your heel brake to the chassis, check these are tight so that the brake is secure and does not judder.

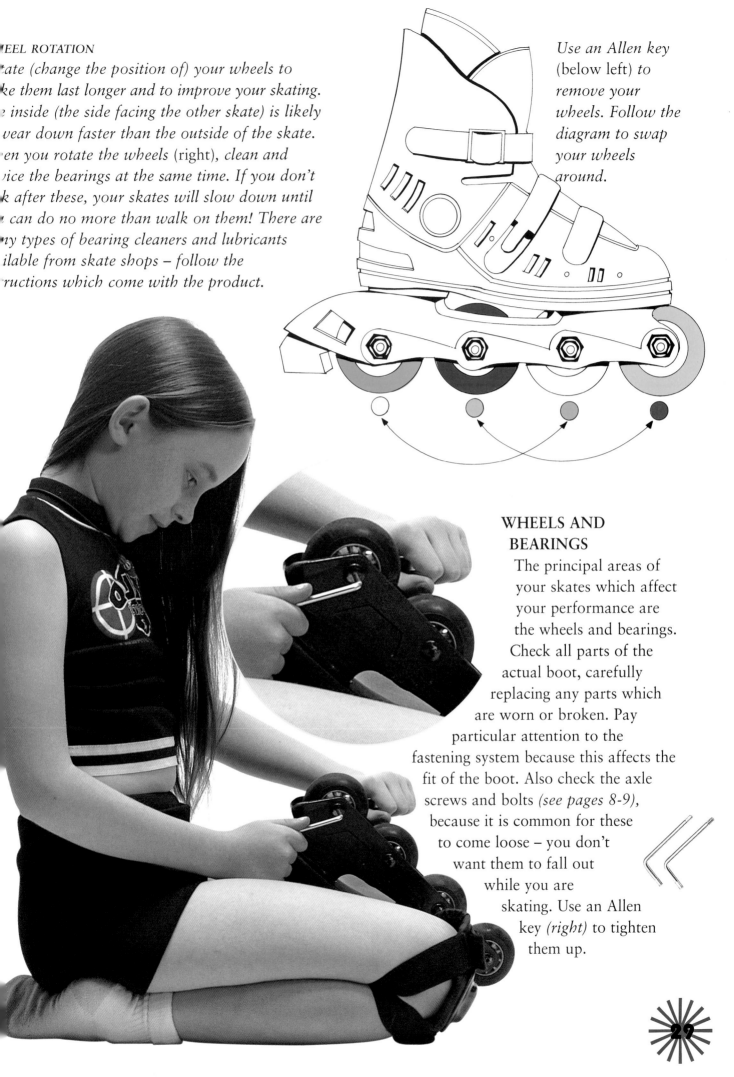

WHEEL ROTATION

...ate (change the position of) your wheels to ...e them last longer and to improve your skating. ... inside (the side facing the other skate) is likely ...wear down faster than the outside of the skate. ...en you rotate the wheels (right), *clean and* ...ice the bearings at the same time. If you don't ...k after these, your skates will slow down until ... can do no more than walk on them! There are ...ny types of bearing cleaners and lubricants ...ilable from skate shops – follow the ...ructions which come with the product.

Use an Allen key (below left) to remove your wheels. Follow the diagram to swap your wheels around.

WHEELS AND BEARINGS

The principal areas of your skates which affect your performance are the wheels and bearings. Check all parts of the actual boot, carefully replacing any parts which are worn or broken. Pay particular attention to the fastening system because this affects the fit of the boot. Also check the axle screws and bolts *(see pages 8-9)*, because it is common for these to come loose – you don't want them to fall out while you are skating. Use an Allen key *(right)* to tighten them up.

Streetwise and safe

Apart from wearing all of your pads, including your helmet, every time you skate, you should also be very careful where you skate – especially when you are learning. Find a place which is smooth and level – sta away from slopes and hills. It should also be well awa from traffic and pedestrians. Public parks where skati is allowed and cycle paths are good places to start. St away from pavements near roads and streets until you are able to stop and control your speed.

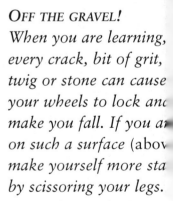

STAIRS AND KERBS
When learning, slow down before stepping up or down kerbs or stairs (right). Lean forwards over the kerb before stepping up. Practising skating on one foot will help you with kerbs, as you need to support all your weight on one skate. If you are unsure, remove both your skates to go up and down stairs.

OFF THE GRAVEL!
When you are learning, every crack, bit of grit, twig or stone can cause your wheels to lock and make you fall. If you ar on such a surface (abov make yourself more sta by scissoring your legs.

LOOKS GOOD
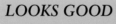
For some skaters, skating is about more than a pair of skates. It's about a comb in the back pocket, a baseball cap, the right T-shirt, a skater's bag, a spare wheel hanging on a chain... *(left)*. But for other skaters, it's just the skating that matters!

HILLS
Only attempt hills (right) when you have perfected your speed control and stopping skills. If you are a beginner, take off your skates and walk – it's much safer!

Skate Speak

"Aggressive" skating
Skating which uses props such
as ramps and rails. It is also
called extreme or stunt skating.

Airs
Jumps or tricks in which you
leave the ground.

Allen key
A tool which is used to remove
the wheels from skates. An
Allen key can also be used
to tighten up the screws and
bolts on skates.

Bearing
A round object which helps a
wheel to spin.

Chassis
The bottom part of an in-line
skate which holds the wheels.

Coping
The point on a ramp where the
"vert" meets the deck.

Deck
The platform area on a ramp.

"Duck" walk
The small practice steps taken
by a beginner.

Fakie
To land or to skate backwards.

Freestyle
A form of recreational skating
with tricks. It is often
performed to music.

Gliding
The free-rolling of skates.

Grind Plates
Plates which are attached to
skates to perform grinds.

Grinds
Sliding with in-line skates on
kerbs, handrails and ledges.

Half-pipe
A ramp which looks similar to
a large pipe cut in half.

In-line hockey
Hockey on in-line skates.

Off-road skating
Skating on rocky terrain.

Pads
Essential protective covering
for elbows and knees. It can
also refer to wrist guards.

Quads
Roller skates with four wheels
arranged in a rectangle.

Quarter-pipe
A ramp which resembles the
shape of a pipe cut into
a quarter.

Ramps
Launches for tricks and jumps.
They include half-pipes,
quarter-pipes and "verts".

Recreational skating
In-line skating for fun.

Scissoring
The position in which one
leg is placed in front of the
other leg.

Sessioning
Spending time skating on
particular ramps or rails.

Spacers
A spacer is a piece of plastic or
metal which holds the bearings
at a fixed distance from
each other.

Speed skating
In-line skating for speed.

Striding
The combination of stroking
and gliding.

Stroking
The push and thrust from the
trailing leg to power movement.

Swizzle
A skating movement in which
your wheels stay in contact
with the ground.

Thrust
The pushing action of the
trailing skate to create forward
movement.

Vert
The part of a ramp which
is vertical.

Index

Photo Credits: *Abbreviations: t-top, m-middle, b-bottom, r-right, l-left, c-centre*

Front cover, 2, 3, 8-9 all, 10-11 all, 12-13 all, 14-15 all, 16m, 18-19 all, 20-21 all, 22 all, 23l, 24b, 26bl, 28mr, 29-30 all – Roger Vlitos; 1 – Andy Critchlow/Inline Skatermag; 4-5, 25bl, 27 & m – Frank Spooner Pictures; 6l, 7b, 17m & 27b – Archie King/Skaters Paradise; 6r, 6-7, 17t & 26r – Sandy Chalmers/Inline Skatermag; 7t – Graham Burkitt/Inline Skatermag; 16t – Rob Tysall; 23tc & 24-25– Paul Rickelton; 26tl – Brian Wood/Inline Skatermag; 28t & ml – Hulton Getty Collection.

The publishers would like to thank Archie and Mathew King and everyone at Skaters Paradise London, for their help and co-operation in the preparation of this book.